CROSSING BORDERS

By Remo Vinciguerra

Piano Book 3

Editorial Consultants:
Anne Applin and Geoffrey Pratley

EDITION PETERS

LONDON · FRANKFURT/M. · LEIPZIG · NEW YORK

CROSSING BORDERS

This progressive new series is intended to enable the developing pianist to cross the often artificial 'border' between classical and popular music. Most of the pieces are in a popular idiom, but a classical spirit or framework can also be recognized in much of the music. The characteristic jazz concept of the 'blue' 3rd and 5th is introduced in the first volume, and in general the rhythmic, melodic and harmonic fingerprints of a wide range of popular styles are presented and developed throughout the volumes. In accordance with the relative freedom typical of popular music, many interpretative decisions, especially concerning dynamics, are left to the player. Tempo indications are for guidance only, and need not be taken too literally. Pedalling is sometimes suggested, but might also be used to good effect in many other places.

The sequence of volumes corresponds in broad terms with standard grading systems.

This edition licensed by permission of Edizioni Curci S.r.l. – Galleria del Corso, 4-20122 Milano.

Pieces 1, 5 originally from *Ciao, Piano!* by Remo Vinciguerra.
Copyright 1995 by Edizioni Curci, Milano.

Pieces 2, 3, 8, 10 originally from *Tempi Moderni* by Remo Vinciguerra.
Copyright 1995 by Edizioni Curci, Milano.

Pieces 4, 6, 9, 11, 12, 15 originally from *I Preludi Colorati* by Remo Vinciguerra.
Copyright 1995 by Edizioni Curci, Milano.

Pieces 7, 13 originally from *Il Mio Primo Concerto* by Remo Vinciguerra.
Copyright 1998 by Edizioni Curci, Milano.

Piece 14 originally from *Pianolandia* by Remo Vinciguerra.
Copyright 1991 by Edizioni Curci, Milano.

Original artwork by Kate Hawley

Peters Edition Limited
Hinrichsen House
10-12 Baches Street
London
N1 6DN

First published 2002 by Hinrichsen Edition, Peters Edition Limited, London

Printed in Great Britain by Halstan & Co. Ltd, Amersham, Bucks., England

CONTENTS

Maypole

1.

Edition Peters No. 7642
This collection © 2002 Hinrichsen Edition, Peters Edition Limited, London.
Printed under licence from Edizioni Curci S.r.l., Milano.

On the Road

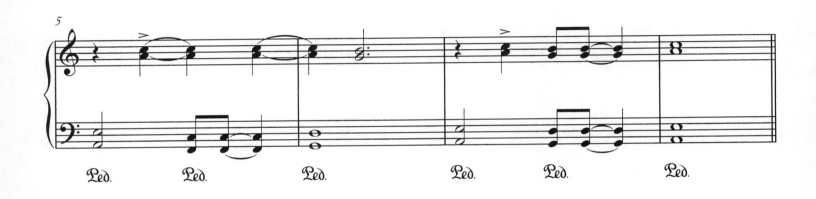

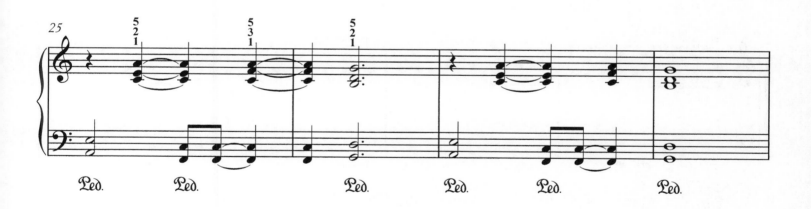

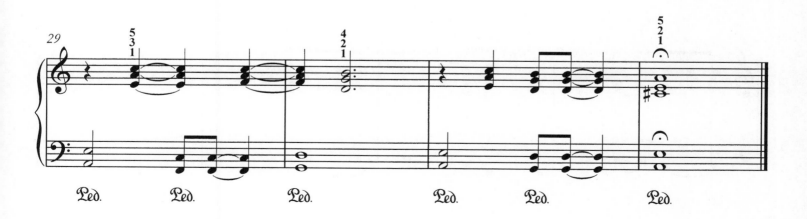

Weekend

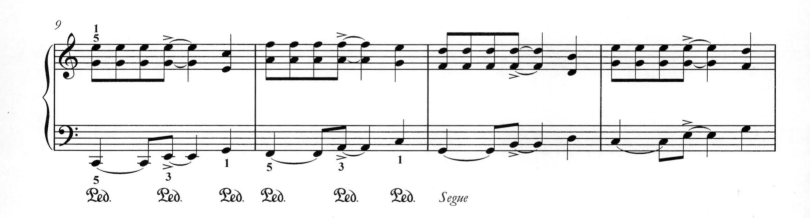

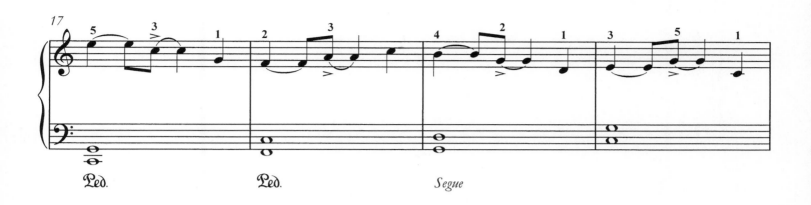

River Flow

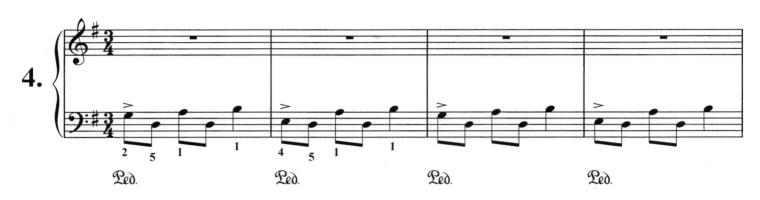

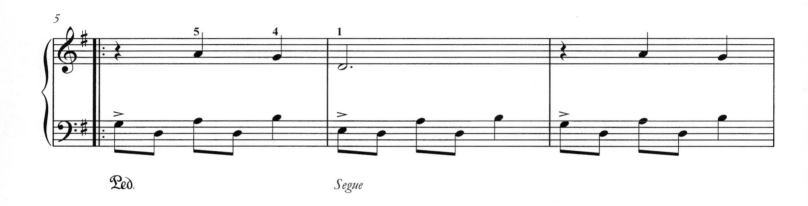

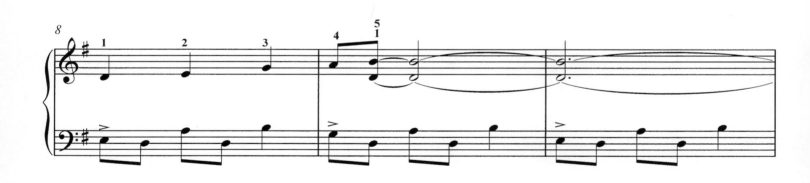

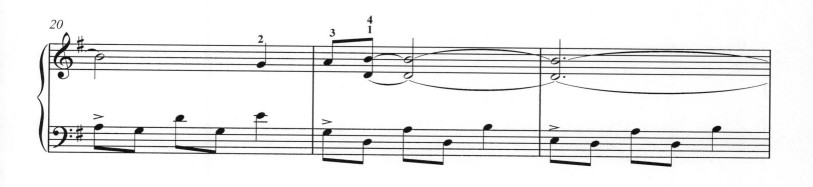

Rall.

Moonstruck

Prelude

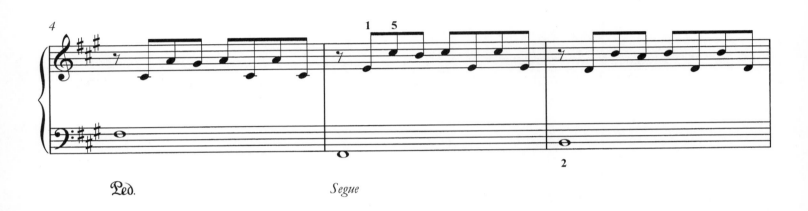

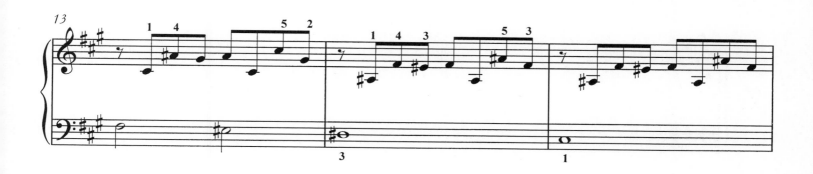

Rall.

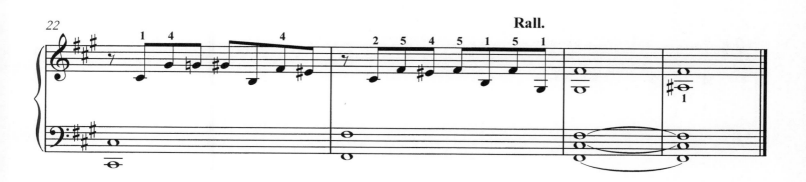

Old Times

Maracas

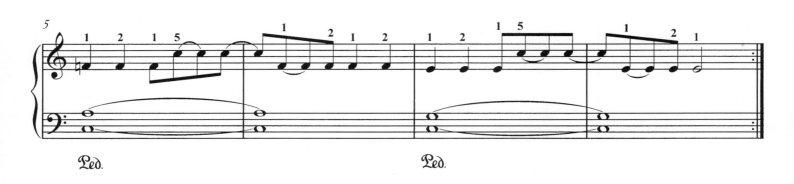

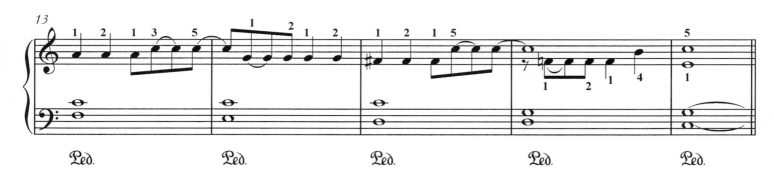

Lazy Day

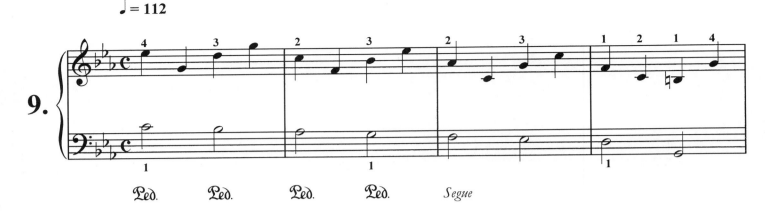

Surprise!

Distant Shore

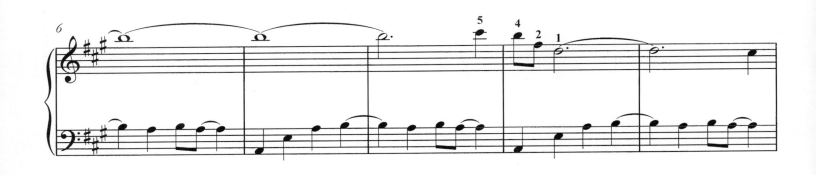

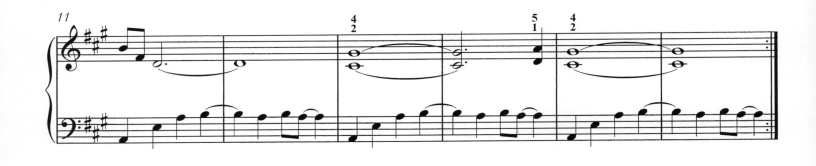

Mountain Rider

12.

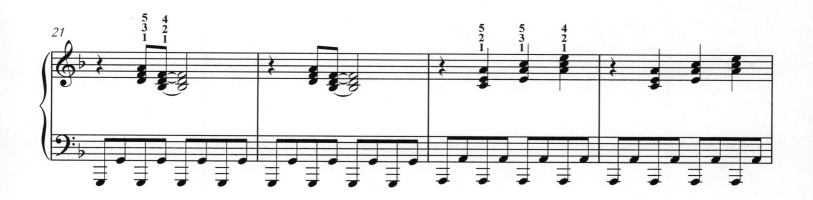

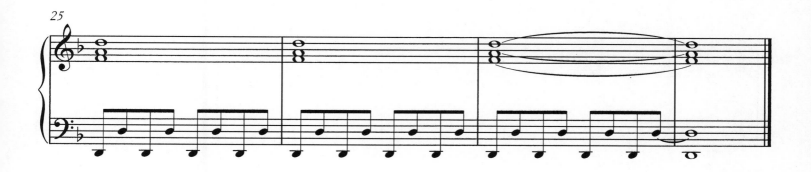

Boogie Bear

13.

Teasing

Bordeaux

15.

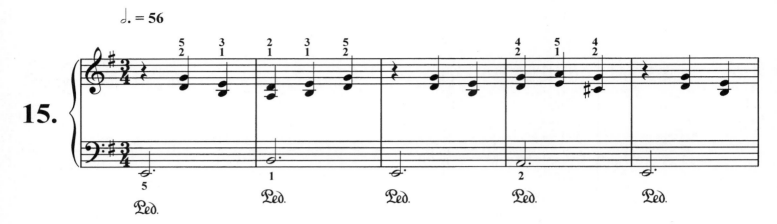

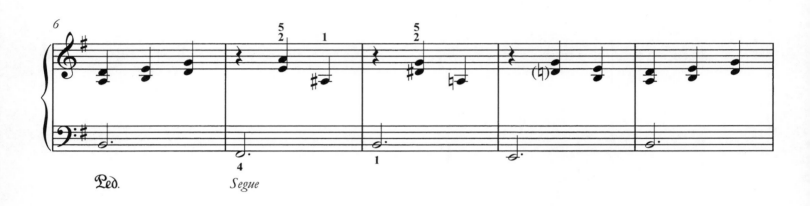

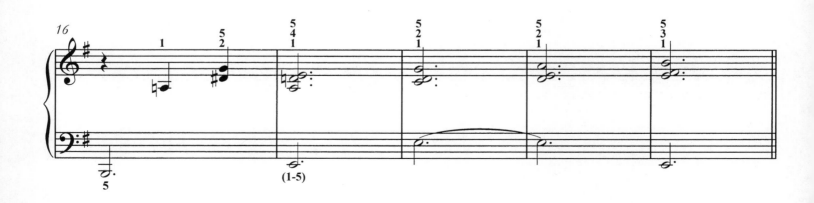

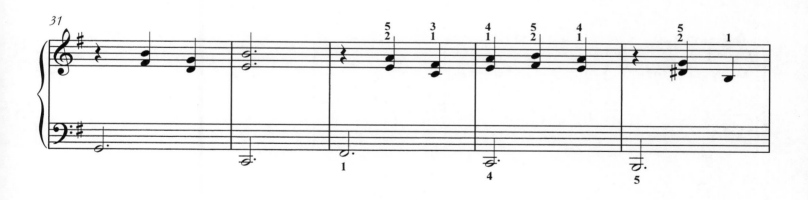

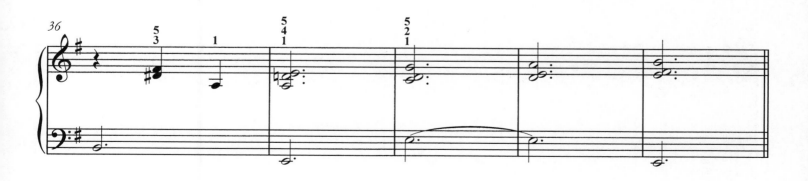

VARIATION

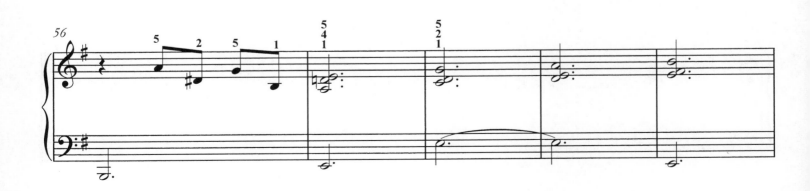

CONTENTS

ISBN 978-0-9931316-8-4
Published by EVC Music Publications

SUTRA

For Elena

Melanie Spanswick

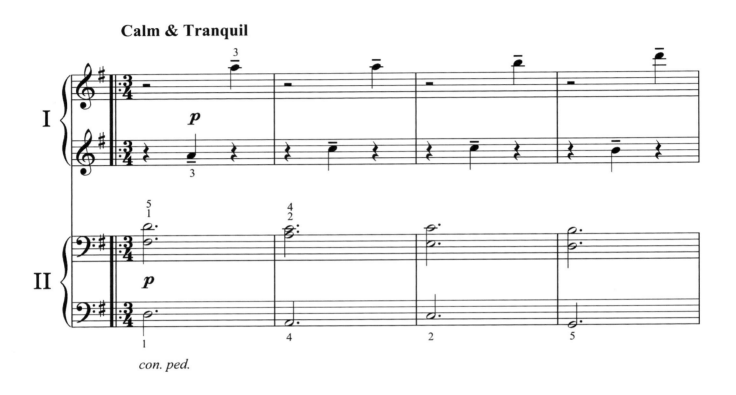

DATE IN MIND

Melanie Spanswick

LIGHT

Melanie Spanswick

SAMSARA

Melanie Spanswick

5

FLOATING

Melanie Spanswick

Con moto

MISTY RAIN

For Joshua

Melanie Spanswick

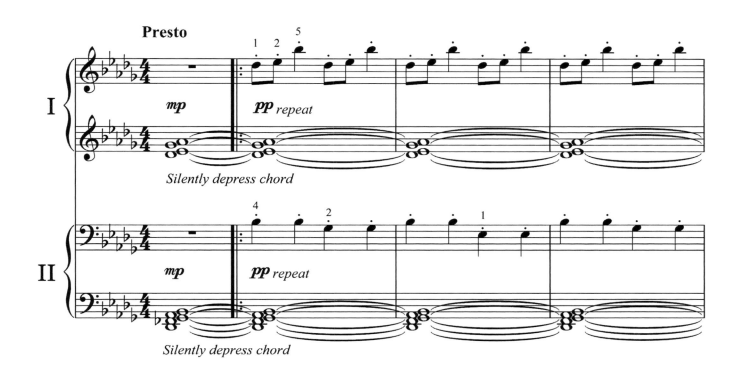

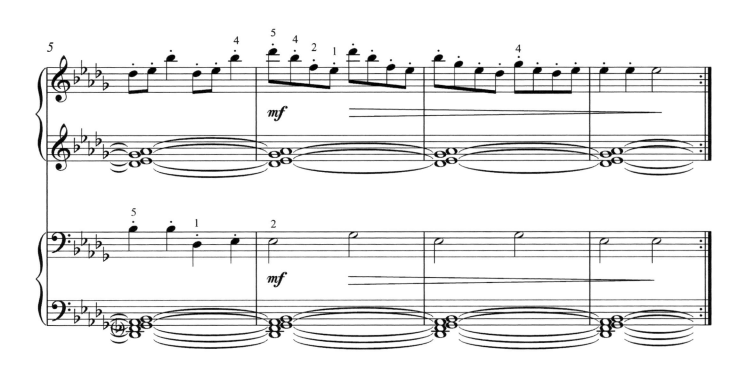

BLACK SQUARE

Melanie Spanswick

Con moto

ANDANTE

Melanie Spanswick

At a walking pace

HOPSCOTCH

For Holly

Melanie Spanswick

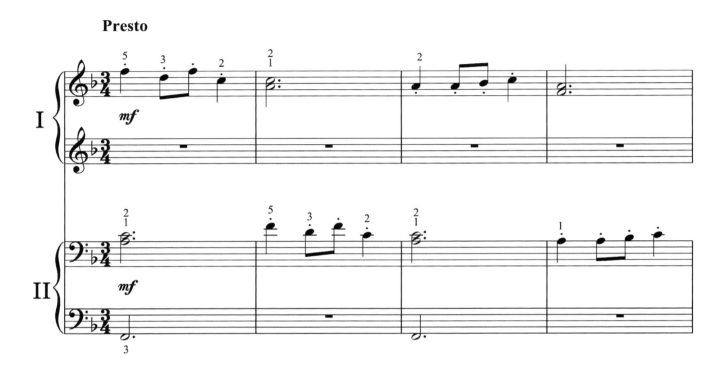

QUICK CHAT

For Nick

Melanie Spanswick

Allegro Vivace

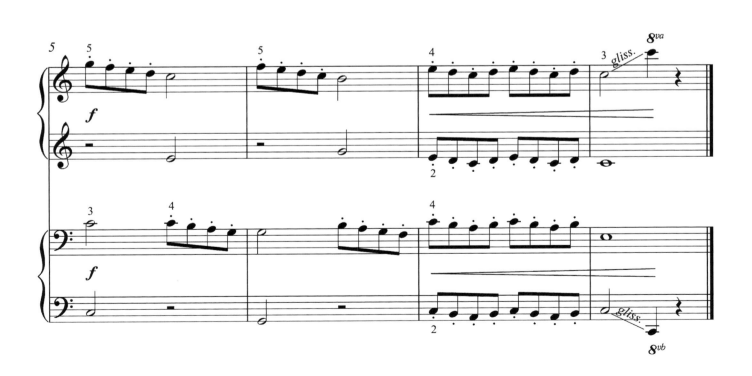

SHANTI SHANTI

Melanie Spanswick

Allegretto

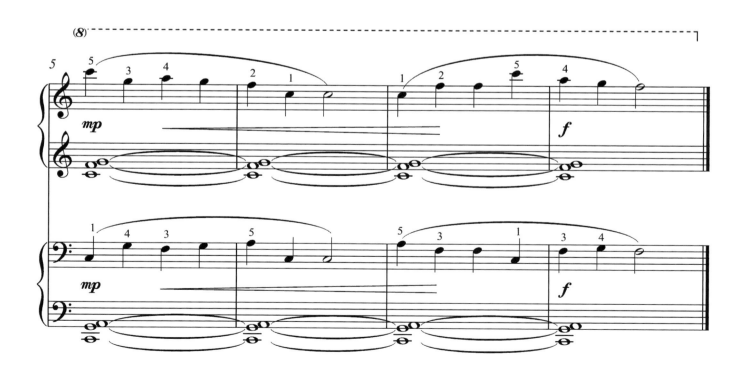